W9-AGB-353

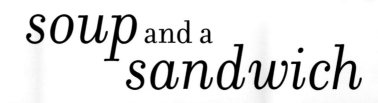

soup and a sandwich

soup and a sandwich

Perfect pairings for satisfying meals

Hannah Miles

photography by Steve Painter

RYLAND PETERS & SMALL
LONDON • NEW YORK

Senior designer Sonya Nathoo
Editors Alice Sambrook and
  Kate Eddison
Head of Production Patricia Harrington
Art director Leslie Harrington
Editorial director Julia Charles
Publisher Cindy Richards

Photographer and prop stylist
  Steve Painter
Food stylist Lucy McKelvie
Indexer Vanessa Bird

First published in 2016 by
Ryland Peters & Small
20–21 Jockey's Fields,
London WC1R 4BW
and
341 E 116th St
New York NY 10029

www.rylandpeters.com

10 9 8 7 6 5 4 3 2 1

Text © Hannah Miles 2016
Design and photographs
© Ryland Peters & Small 2016

ISBN: 978-1-84975-772-0

The author's moral rights have been
asserted. All rights reserved. No part
of this publication may be reproduced,
stored in a retrieval system or
transmitted in any form or by any
means, electronic, mechanical,
photocopying or otherwise, without
the prior permission of the publisher.

A CIP record for this book is available
from the British Library.
US Library of Congress cataloguing-in-
publication data has been applied for.

Printed and bound in China

Dedication
For Jane and Geoff
and their beautiful
grandson Dylon x

Author's acknowledgments
Heartfelt thanks to the design
and editorial teams at Ryland
Peters and Small and to Steve
and Lucy for the photographs
in this beautiful book. To all my
friends and family who sampled
the soups – you are stars,
particularly Maren and Lucy
who loved the Cheese and
Beer Soup (page 58) the best!

contents

introduction

Who doesn't love soup? Soups are one of the most delicious comfort foods and are so quick and easy to prepare that they offer instant satisfaction. Although soups can be humble, they can also be dressed up to become something spectacular with a little garnish and a flourish of high-hitting flavours. They make ideal quick lunches or suppers and are also great prepare-ahead meals as most of the soups in this book freeze well.

The soups here are all paired with sandwiches, or twists on sandwiches, taking them from appetizer to a complete meal and offering a taste sensation. So in place of the traditional (and rather dull) bread to dip into soup, why not serve a delicious sandwich on the side?

The CLASSIC COMBOS chapter contains all those family favourites, where recipes have been passed down from generation to generation – tomato soup with a melting mozzarella panini, pea soup with American-style biscuits or the classic leek and potato, served with cheese toasties. There is also the Parisian favourite of onion soup served with a French twist on rarebit made with Gruyère cheese. My personal favourite recipe also appears in this chapter – the classic American Reuben with salt beef, sauerkraut, Swiss cheese and Russian dressing paired with a humble vegetable soup, elevating it to a very special meal.

For the more health conscious or to serve on hot days when a lighter broth is called for, the LIGHTER BITES chapter contains a delicate vegetable consommé with asparagus and broad/fava beans with a whipped lemon and mint feta brioche and Japanese miso soup with sushi 'sandwich'. Packed with flavour is the Korean-style beef broth served with a kimchi, beef and cheese toastie on the side. For days when the temperature is rising, serve refreshing chilled strawberry gazpacho with pickled peppers on a serrano ham and olive tapenade sandwich.

The next chapter contains HOME-COOKED COMFORTS – those that will pick you up when you are in need of comfort food. Whenever I am poorly I always find the chicken noodle broth makes me feel better – this chapter has one made with tarragon giving it a delicious aniseed kick. There is also a warming Costa Rican black bean soup with cornbread muffins and a rich red pepper, fennel and ouzo soup inspired by my travels to Greece and Cyprus with a prawn/shrimp 'saganaki' pitta – the sunshine flavours work as the ultimate 'pick-me-up'.

For richer soups, the INDULGENT TREATS chapter contains delicious langoustine bisque, rich with brandy and cream served with seafood rolls, similar to the American classic lobster rolls. There is also a butternut squash soup served with pretzel club sandwiches filled with Thanksgiving favourites turkey and cranberry and topped with Swiss cheese. For those with more adventurous taste buds, there is a Hungarian-inspired goulash soup accompanied by a meatball sub and a cheese and beer soup served with quesadillas.

With flavours from all around the world, the recipes in this book will have something for everyone – whether your preference is a delicate broth or a bowl of hearty creamy soup. All you need is a pan and blender and some good fresh ingredients and you will be creating delicious meals in no time!

classic combos

Roasted tomato soup with pesto drizzle and melting mozzarella panini

700 g/1^1/$_2$ lb. cherry
   tomatoes
olive oil, to drizzle
1 tablespoon balsamic glaze
   or vinegar
1 teaspoon caster/granulated
   sugar
800 ml/generous 3^1/$_4$ cups
   vegetable stock
150 ml/^{2}/$_3$ cup single/light
   cream
a handful of fresh basil leaves
salt and pepper, to season
pesto, to drizzle

For the panini
4 panini rolls
1 tablespoon olive oil
2 heaped tablespoons pesto
2 large balls of mozzarella,
   thinly sliced
a handful of fresh basil leaves

a panini press (optional)

Serves 4

Sometimes a soup can have very few ingredients but still be bursting with flavour. Here roasting the tomatoes with a sprinkling of salt and a drizzle of balsamic vinegar gives them a real zing. Serve with a delicious mozzarella panini on the side, complete with pesto drizzle.

Preheat the oven to 180°C (350°F) Gas 4.

Place the tomatoes in a roasting pan. Drizzle over the olive oil and balsamic glaze or vinegar, sprinkle with the sugar and season well with salt and pepper. Shake the pan well so all the tomatoes are coated. Roast for about 20–30 minutes until the tomatoes are soft.

Place the tomatoes and the roasting liquid from the pan into a saucepan and add the stock. Simmer for 15 minutes and then place in a blender or food processor and blitz until very smooth. Pass through a sieve/strainer to remove the tomato skins. Add the cream and basil to the tomato soup and blitz again. Taste for seasoning and add more salt and pepper to your taste. Keep the soup warm while you prepare the sandwiches.

Cut the panini rolls in half. Brush the outsides with a thin layer of olive oil. Spread the inside of each roll with pesto, cover with thin slices of mozzarella and top with a few basil leaves. Replace the top of each panini roll and then heat in the panini press for about 3–5 minutes until the cheese starts to melt. If you do not have a panini press, place the panini in a frying pan/skillet and fry gently until the cheese starts to melt and bubble. You may need to cook them in batches depending on the size of your pan.

Swirl a little pesto on top of the soup if you like and serve straight away with the panini.

1 onion, finely chopped
1 tablespoon olive oil
1 garlic clove, sliced
500 g/1 lb. 2 oz. frozen peas
1 litre/quart vegetable stock
125 ml/$^1/_2$ cup milk or cream
salt and pepper, to season

For the biscuits
225 g/1$^3/_4$ cups self-raising/
    self-rising flour, sifted
$^1/_4$ teaspoon each salt and
    freshly ground pepper
$^1/_2$ teaspoon baking powder
60 g/$^1/_2$ stick salted butter,
    chilled and cubed
60 g/2 oz. strong/sharp
    cheddar cheese, grated
1 heaped teaspoon
    wholegrain mustard
125 ml/$^1/_2$ cup buttermilk
1 egg, beaten, for glazing

To serve
50 g/3$^1/_2$ tablespoons soft
    butter
Worcestershire sauce, to taste
1 teaspoon wholegrain
    mustard
4 slices thick-cut ham

6-cm/5$^1/_2$-inch round cutter

*large baking sheet, greased
    and lined*

Serves 4

Classic pea soup with warm buttermilk biscuits

Fear not those of you to whom a 'biscuit' means a sweet cookie, as these are my version of the classic American biscuits, which are warm scones – a perfect accompaniment for soup. Best eaten on the day they are made, they are served here with a mustard butter and thickly carved ham.

Preheat the oven to 180°C (350°F) Gas 4.

For the biscuits, place the flour, salt, pepper and baking powder in a large mixing bowl. Rub the chilled butter into the flour lightly with your fingertips until it resembles fine breadcrumbs. Add the grated cheese, mustard and buttermilk and mix to form a soft dough. Add a little more buttermilk or regular milk if the mixture is too dry.

On a lightly floured surface, gently roll out the dough to 2.5 cm/1 inch thickness and cut out the biscuits with the 6-cm/5½-inch cutter. Place the biscuits on the baking sheet so that they are almost touching. Brush the tops with the beaten egg and sprinkle with a little extra grated cheese if liked. Bake for 25–30 minutes until golden brown and the biscuits sound hollow when you tap them. Leave on the baking sheet for 5 minutes, then transfer to a rack to cool.

While the biscuits are baking, make the soup. Add the chopped onion to the pan with the oil and fry over a gentle heat until the onion is soft and translucent. Add the garlic and fry until it just starts to turn golden brown, taking care that it does not burn. Add a few drops of water to the pan if the onion and garlic start to brown too much. Add the peas and stock to the pan and simmer for about 5 minutes until the peas are just soft. Add the milk or cream and blitz until very smooth in a blender or food processor. Return to the pan and season to taste with salt and pepper.

For the mustard butter, whisk the soft butter, a dash of Worcestershire sauce and mustard together. Cut the warm biscuits in half, spread with the butter and place a slice of ham into each. Serve the soup hot with the warm filled biscuits and tuck in straight away.

Leek and potato soup with wholegrain mustard cheddar toasties

350 g/³/₄ lb. leeks, trimmed
50 g/3¹/₂ tablespoons butter
350 g/³/₄ lb. new potatoes or white potatoes
800 ml/generous 3¹/₄ cups vegetable stock
2 teaspoons wholegrain mustard
salt and pepper, to season
vegetable oil, for frying

For the cheddar toasties
soft butter, for spreading
8 slices brioche or white bread
2 teaspoons wholegrain mustard
200 g/7 oz. cheddar cheese, grated

a sandwich maker or panini press (optional)

Serves 4

Leek and potato soup is one of the most comforting soups I know. Creamy and luxurious with a hint of mustard, here it is served with classic toasted cheese sandwiches. Use brioche, as the sweetness of the bread with the tangy mustard and cheese really complements the soup.

Reserve about one-third of one of the leeks to make the fried leeks for the topping. Slice the remaining leeks and rinse them well. Place the leeks in a large saucepan with the butter and fry over a gentle heat until the leeks are soft.

If you are using white potatoes, peel them and cut them into chunks and add to the pan. If you are using new potatoes, simply halve them and place them in the pan with their skins on. Add the stock and mustard to the pan and simmer for about 25–30 minutes until the potatoes are soft. Season with salt and pepper.

Blend the soup in a food processor until smooth. If you prefer a chunkier soup, blend half of the soup, leaving half of the mixture chunky to add texture.

For the leek garnish, finely slice the reserved leeks into very thin strips. Heat the vegetable oil in a small pan and fry the leeks until they are crispy. Remove from the oil and drain on paper towels. Sprinkle with a little salt to season.

For the sandwiches, butter one side of each slice of bread and then spread a thin layer of mustard over the other side of each slice. Place one-quarter of the cheese on top of four mustard-covered slices and top with the other slices of bread, with the mustard on the inside. Place each sandwich in a sandwich toaster or a panini press and cook until golden brown. If you do not have a sandwich toaster or panini press, place the panini in a frying pan/skillet and fry gently until the cheese starts to melt and bubble (you don't need to add any oil as the bread is buttered).

Serve the soup in bowls or mugs, sprinkled with the crispy leeks. Serve the hot sandwiches alongside.

1 onion, finely chopped

1 stick/rib celery, trimmed
  and chopped

1 garlic clove, finely chopped

1 tablespoon olive oil

1 leek

30 g/2 tablespoons butter

3 carrots, peeled and
  chopped

2 parsnips, peeled and
  chopped

800 ml/generous 3^{1}/$_{4}$ cups
  vegetable stock

For the Russian dressing

2 egg yolks

1 teaspoon Dijon mustard

1 tablespoon white wine
  vinegar

200 ml/^{3}/$_{4}$ cup mild olive oil

1 tablespoon horseradish

1 tablespoon tomato ketchup

salt and pepper, to season

For the Reuben sandwiches

8 slices rye bread

8–12 slices salt beef or
  pastrami

4 tablespoons prepared
  sauerkraut

8 slices Swiss cheese (such
  as Emmental)

a sandwich press

Serves 4

Vegetable soup with Reuben sandwiches

This is comfort food at its best — a thick, wholesome vegetable soup served with classic New York Reuben sandwiches. I adore a Reuben sandwich — there is something so indulgent about tangy horseradish mayo, sauerkraut and salt beef all warm with melting gooey cheese.

Begin by preparing the Russian dressing. Place the egg yolks, mustard and vinegar in a blender or food processor and blitz. With the blades on a slow speed, very slowly drizzle in the olive oil and whisk until the mayonnaise is thick. Carefully fold through the horseradish and ketchup and season with salt and pepper. Store in a jar in the refrigerator until needed.

For the soup, add the onion, celery and garlic to a large saucepan with the olive oil and fry over a gentle heat until soft and the onion is translucent. Trim the ends of the leek, discard any damaged leaves and finely slice. Rinse well to remove any dirt and then add to the pan with the butter. Cook gently for about 5 minutes until the leeks have sweated down and are soft. Add the chopped carrots and parsnips to the pan with the stock and simmer for about 15 minutes until the carrots and parsnips are soft. The actual cooking time will depend on the size of the vegetables. Once the vegetables are soft, carefully transfer to a blender or food processor and blitz until the soup is smooth. Return to the pan and keep warm until you are ready to serve.

For the sandwiches, lightly butter the outside of the rye bread, then turn over on a board and spread a layer of the Russian dressing over four of the slices. Top with the salt beef slices. Heat the sauerkraut to evaporate the liquid and then sprinkle a spoonful over the beef in each sandwich. Top with two slices of cheese and a further spoonful of dressing and then top each sandwich with the remaining buttered rye slices. Toast each sandwich in the sandwich press or in a griddle pan until warm and the cheese has melted.

Serve the soup with sandwiches on the side for a delicious lunch or supper.

2 tablespoons butter
1 tablespoon olive oil
1 shallot, finely chopped
250 g/9 oz. chestnut
   mushrooms, trimmed
   and cleaned with a brush
   or soft cloth
250 g/9 oz. button
   mushrooms, trimmed
   and cleaned with a brush
   or soft cloth
1 sprig of thyme
1 sprig of rosemary
1 teaspoon porcini
   mushroom paste (optional)
$^1/_2$ teaspoon finely grated
   lemon zest
75 ml/5 tablespoons sweet
   sherry
800 ml/generous 3$^1/_4$ cups
   chicken or vegetable stock
salt and pepper, to season

For the roasted garlic purée
2 whole garlic bulbs
1 tablespoon olive oil

For the sandwiches
1 focaccia loaf
100 g/3$^1/_2$ oz. cream cheese
a handful of rocket/arugula,
   leaves and flowers
50 g/2 oz. bresaola
shavings of Parmesan cheese

Serves 4

Garlic mushroom soup
with bresaola-filled focaccia

This soup is dedicated to my wonderful culinary mentor Giancarlo Caldesi who taught me in his restaurant how to cook mushrooms so that they 'smell of the forest'. Cooked in butter with herbs and roasted garlic, these mushrooms will make your kitchen smell sensational.

Begin by roasting the garlic. You can do this the day before and store in the refrigerator.

Preheat the oven to 180°C (350°F) Gas 4. Place the whole garlic bulbs in a roasting pan and drizzle with olive oil so the skin is lightly coated. Roast for about 30–40 minutes until the bulbs feel soft when you press them. Remove from the oven and leave to cool.

For the soup, place the butter and olive oil in the pan and add the finely chopped shallot. Sauté for about 3–5 minutes until the shallot is soft and translucent. Add the mushrooms to the pan with the thyme and rosemary. Cut the roasted garlic bulbs in half and squeeze out the soft garlic purée, making sure that you do not include any of the skin. Add one-quarter of the garlic purée to the pan and reserve the remainder for the sandwiches. Season with salt and pepper and, over a gentle heat, sauté the mushrooms for about 5 minutes until the mixture smells very earthy. Remove the thyme and rosemary sprigs.

Add the porcini paste to the pan with the lemon zest, then pour in the sherry and stock and simmer for 15 minutes. Reserve a few whole mushrooms to garnish, then blitz the soup to a smooth consistency in a blender or food processor. Season to taste.

To prepare the sandwiches, lightly warm the focaccia bread, then cut into four wedges and slice each one in half horizontally. Spread the base of each sandwich with a generous layer of cream cheese. Top with some rocket/arugula leaves and the bresaola, then spread the top of each sandwich with a little of the garlic purée. Add a few shavings of Parmesan.

Pour the soup into bowls, garnish with the reserved whole mushrooms and serve with the sandwiches on the side.

Carrot and ginger soup with hummus and pickled carrot baguettes

1 tablespoon olive oil
1 small onion, finely chopped
1 tablespoon grated fresh
    ginger
500 g/1 lb. 2 oz. carrots,
    peeled and chopped
1 litre/quart chicken or
    vegetable stock
25 g/1 oz. fresh coriander/
    cilantro leaves
juice of 1 large orange
salt and pepper, to season

For the carrot pickle
1 carrot, peeled and trimmed
2 tablespoons white wine
    vinegar
2 teaspoons caster/
    granulated sugar
1 teaspoon cumin seeds
pinch of salt

For the sandwiches
1 medium baguette
150 g/5$\frac{1}{2}$ oz. hummus
a handful of spinach leaves
a handful of fresh coriander/
    cilantro leaves

Serves 4

Although carrots may not make you see in the dark, they can certainly offer you a comforting 'pick-me-up' in the form of this earthy carrot and ginger soup. The soup is accompanied by a crusty baguette filled with delicious hummus and crunchy carrot pickle. If you like carrots, this will be one of your favourite lunches.

For the pickle, use a swivel peeler to make long strips of carrot. Place in a bowl with the vinegar and sugar. In a dry frying pan/skillet heat the cumin seeds until they start to pop, taking care that you do not burn them. Add to the bowl with the salt and stir so that the sugar and salt dissolve and the carrot strips are all coated in the pickling juices. Leave for about 1 hour to soak.

For the soup, heat the olive oil in a large saucepan and fry the chopped onion until soft and translucent. Add the grated ginger and fry for a further 1–2 minutes. Add the chopped carrots to the pan with the stock, coriander/cilantro leaves and orange juice and simmer until the carrots are soft. Place in a blender or food processor and blitz to a smooth purée. Return to the pan to keep warm and season with salt and pepper to taste.

When you are ready to serve, pour the soup into warm bowls. Cut the baguette into four portions and slice each one in half horizontally. Fill with the hummus, spinach and coriander/cilantro leaves. Drain the pickling liquid from the carrots and add some of the carrot ribbons to each sandwich. Serve straight away.

French onion soup with Gruyère rarebits

600 g/1 lb. 5 oz. onions
50 g/3½ tablespoons butter
1 tablespoon olive oil
1 teaspoon white sugar
125 ml/½ cup sherry or
    brandy
800 ml/generous 3¼ cups
    beef stock
salt and pepper, to season

For the rarebits
200 g/7 oz. Gruyère cheese,
    grated (or other hard
    cheese such as cheddar
    or Emmental)
1 egg, beaten
2 teaspoons wholegrain
    mustard
1 tablespoon Worcestershire
    sauce
8 thin slices brown bread,
    or 4 square 'sandwich thins'

a mandoline (optional)

Serves 4

French onion soup is my go-to 'therapy' cooking. In order to maximize the flavour of this soup, it is really important to caramelize the onions until golden brown, so that they release a rich sweetness into the soup. As this requires you to continuously stir for some time, pour yourself a large glass of wine and lose yourself in your thoughts as you do so!

Peel the onions and then slice them very finely either using a sharp knife or a mandoline. Place the onions in a heavy-based saucepan with the butter and olive oil. Season with a pinch of salt and sweat the onions down over a gentle heat until they become soft and translucent and start to caramelize. Take care that they do not burn as this will add bitterness to the soup. Cooking the onions will take around 15 minutes. Add a good grind of coarse black pepper to the pan with the sugar and stir for a few minutes further.

Add the sherry or brandy to the pan and simmer for a few minutes to cook off the alcohol. Add the stock to the pan and simmer for 5 minutes, then taste for seasoning, adding a little more salt and pepper if needed. Keep warm while you prepare the sandwiches. If you prefer a smooth soup, you can blend it at this stage, although traditionally this soup is not blended.

For the sandwiches, mix the grated cheese with the egg, mustard and Worcestershire sauce. Preheat the grill/broiler and cut each sandwich thin in half. Lightly toast the four bottom halves of the sandwich thins. Spread the cheese mixture over the bottom halves and place under the grill/broiler together with the empty top halves, cut-side up, and grill/broil until the cheese is melted and golden brown and the tops are lightly toasted. Watch carefully as the tops may cook quicker – if so, remove them from the grill/broiler slightly sooner than the cheese-covered halves.

To serve, pour the soup into four bowls, place the toasted tops on the rarebits and serve straight away.

lighter bites

Broccoli soup with blue cheese and pine nut croissants

1 tablespoon olive oil
1 onion, finely chopped
1 garlic clove, finely sliced
1 head of broccoli (approx. 300 g/10$\frac{1}{2}$ oz. in weight)
1 litre/quart chicken or vegetable stock
salt and pepper, to season
cream, to swirl (optional)

For the croissants
4 plain all-butter croissants
200 g/7 oz. gorgonzola dolce or other soft blue cheese
50 g/scant $\frac{1}{2}$ cup pine nuts

Serves 4

Broccoli is one of the super vegetables that can really boost your immune system so I like to make this soup when I am feeling under the weather – when blended it is an uplifting bright green colour. Broccoli goes really well with blue cheese. It is perfect served with warm stuffed croissants filled with tangy cheese and the crunch of toasted pine nuts.

Begin by preparing the soup. Heat the oil in a large saucepan and fry the onion until soft and translucent. Add the garlic and fry until lightly golden brown. Cut the broccoli into small florets and discard the large stem. Add the florets to the pan with the stock and simmer for about 10–15 minutes until the broccoli is just soft but is still a vibrant green colour. If you overcook it, it will start to lose its colour. Blitz the soup to a smooth consistency in a blender or food processor. Return to the pan and season with salt and pepper to taste.

Preheat the oven to 180°C (350°F) Gas 4.

Cut each of the croissants in half horizontally and place a slice or two of the cheese into each. Toast the pine nuts in a dry frying pan/skillet over a gentle heat until they are lightly golden brown and then sprinkle on top of the cheese. Replace the top of each croissant and wrap in a foil parcel. Bake in the oven for about 5 minutes until the cheese starts to melt.

To serve, pour the soup into warm bowls, swirl with a little cream if liked and add freshly ground pepper to garnish. Serve with the warm croissants on the side.

1 large tomato, quartered

2 carrots, peeled and
chopped

1 large leek, trimmed, rinsed
and chopped

1 stick/rib of celery, trimmed
and chopped

1 garlic clove, chopped

1 onion, quartered

75 ml/5 tablespoons Noilly
Prat vermouth or sherry

1 tablespoon fresh mint

1 sprig of tarragon

2 teaspoons Worcestershire
sauce

100 g/1 cup asparagus tips

100 g/generous $^3/_4$ cup
shelled broad/fava beans

50 g/generous $^1/_3$ cup frozen
petit pois or peas

salt and pepper, to season

For the brioche toasts

4 slices brioche

grated zest of 1 lemon, plus
a little extra to garnish

100 g/3$^1/_2$ oz. cream cheese

100 g/3$^1/_2$ oz. feta cheese

1 tablespoon freshly chopped
mint, plus a little extra to
garnish

olive oil, to drizzle

Serves 4

Spring vegetable broth with whipped lemon and mint feta brioche

Making consommé can seem daunting, even to chefs, as the perfect bowl needs to be crystal clear. No need to worry though as this recipe is simplicity itself. It looks so pretty with asparagus tips and peas floating in it and every spoonful is full of the fresh taste of spring.

Place 1 litre/quart of water in a large saucepan and add the tomato, carrots, leek and celery with the garlic and onion. Season with salt and pepper. Add the Noilly Prat, mint and tarragon and simmer for about 30–40 minutes until the vegetables are all soft and the liquid is reduced. Strain through a fine mesh sieve/strainer. Do not press down on the vegetables as this can add impurities to the soup. The soup should be very clear. Stir in the Worcestershire sauce and return the soup to the heat. Trim the asparagus and add to the pan with the broad/fava beans and peas and simmer for about 5 minutes until the asparagus is just cooked. Taste for seasoning, adding a little more salt and pepper if needed.

Toast the slices of brioche until lightly golden brown on both sides. Add the finely grated lemon zest to a mixing bowl with the cream cheese and feta cheese. Add the mint and whisk until smooth. Spread the whipped cheese over the toasts and garnish with a little extra lemon zest and mint if you wish. Drizzle with a little olive oil and serve sprinkled with a little cracked black pepper. Serve straight away with the soup. The soup will store for up to 3 days in the refrigerator, but cook the asparagus, broad/fava beans and peas just before serving.

Miso soup with a sushi 'sandwich'

1 litre/quart dashi or
   vegetable stock
1 tablespoon yellow miso
   paste
1 tablespoon red miso paste
60 ml/¼ cup mirin wine
2 spring onions/scallions
1 tablespoon soy sauce
200 g/7 oz. tofu

For the sushi 'sandwich'
125 g/⅔ cup sushi rice
1 tablespoon sushi vinegar
sheet of dried seaweed
2 large roasted red (bell)
   peppers in brine (such
   as Karyatis)

a sushi mat

Serves 4

Miso is a warming Japanese broth – it takes very little time to prepare as it is made from a fermented soybean, rice or grain paste readily available in supermarkets. Each type of miso has its own flavour so if you enjoy its earthy taste it is worth buying several types and blending them to find your perfect balance. Serve with a fun sushi 'sandwich'.

Begin by preparing the sushi to serve with the soup. Cook the sushi rice following the packet instructions. (The brand I use comes as a boil-in-the-bag variety which you cook for 25 minutes.) Once cooked, tip into a bowl and leave to cool. Stir in the sushi vinegar.

Cut the sheet of seaweed in half so that you have a piece about 20 x 8 cm/8 x 3 inches and place one half on the sushi mat. Cover the seaweed with a thin layer of rice (using half of the rice), pressing it out with your clean fingers. Drain and open out the (bell) peppers so that they are in a single layer and place over the rice in a flat layer. Cover with the remainder of the rice, again pressing it out in a thin layer over the (bell) peppers. Cover with the second sheet of seaweed and fold over the sushi mat and press down so that the layer is compacted.

Remove the sushi mat and, using a very sharp knife, trim the sides of the sushi layer and then cut into 4 triangles to look like sandwiches. Cover with clingfilm/plastic wrap and store in the refrigerator while you make the soup.

For the miso soup, place the stock in a large saucepan with the miso pastes and mirin wine and simmer while stirring to dissolve the pastes. Trim and finely slice the spring onions/scallions and add to the pan. Add the soy sauce. Drain the tofu from any liquid in its packaging and cut into small cubes. Add to the pan and simmer for a further few minutes. Serve straight away with a sushi 'sandwich' on the side.

Korean beef broth with kimchi grilled cheese

500 g/1 lb. 2 oz. beef brisket
1 onion, peeled and chopped
3 spring onions/scallions, trimmed and sliced
2.5-cm/1-inch piece of ginger, peeled and sliced
1 beef stock pot or cube
fresh coriander/cilantro, to garnish
salt and pepper, to season

For the grilled cheese
30 g/2 tablespoons soft butter
8 slices bread
thin slices brisket (from the soup recipe above)
12 slices cheese (such as cheddar or Monterey jack)
4 tablespoons kimchi pickle

Serves 4

Kimchi pickle is a national dish of Korea and in this recipe it is used as a delicious cheese toastie filling along with slices of beef. Kimchi is available to buy from good supermarkets and online, but if you want to try making your own there are recipes available on the internet.

Heat a griddle pan until very hot. Sear the beef on all sides. Place the beef in a large saucepan with 2 litres/quarts water. Add the onion, spring onions/scallions, ginger and stock cube. Simmer for about 2 hours until the liquid has reduced significantly, skimming any fat and impurities from the surface.

Remove the beef and strain the soup through a sieve/strainer – discard the vegetables and retain the liquid. Season with salt and pepper. Allow the liquid to cool and then chill in the refrigerator. Store the beef in the refrigerator as well.

When the soup has chilled and you are ready to eat, remove any fat which has set on the surface of the soup and then reheat in a pan. Cut the beef into very thin slices and place some in the centre of each soup bowl, reserving some for the sandwiches below.

While the soup reheats, make the sandwiches. Butter one side of each slice of bread. On one non-buttered side, place slices of the beef, three slices of cheese and top with a tablespoon of kimchi pickle. Cover with a second slice of bread, butter-side up, and then fry in a griddle pan for about 3 minutes on each side until the cheese has melted and the sandwich is golden brown. Repeat with the remaining sandwiches. Depending on the size of your pan you will probably need to cook the sandwiches in batches.

Pour the warm broth into the bowls and garnish with some coriander/cilantro leaves. Serve with the sandwiches on the side.

2.5-cm/1-inch piece ginger
1 onion, finely sliced
1 garlic clove, finely sliced
1 tablespoon olive oil
2 star anise
1 teaspoon ground cinnamon
$\frac{1}{2}$ teaspoon dried hot pepper
  flakes
1 tablespoon each chopped
  coriander/cilantro and basil
1 tablespoon soy sauce
1 tablespoon fish sauce
1 litre/quart vegetable stock
1 carrot, peeled
2 spring onions/scallions
1 pak choi/bok choy
150 g/5$\frac{1}{2}$ oz. mushrooms
juice of 2 limes
2 teaspoons white sugar
80 g/3 oz. ramen noodles

For the pickles
2 baby corn
2 carrots, peeled
10-cm/4-inch piece cucumber
1 tablespoon each fish sauce,
  wine vinegar and sugar

For the tofu banh mi
1 tablespoon olive oil
200 g/7 oz. tofu
2 tablespoons sweet chilli/
  chili sauce
sprigs of coriander/cilantro
2 small baguettes

Serves 4

Vietnamese vegetable pho with tofu banh mi

Vietnamese cooking is fresh and fragrant with the perfect combination of sweet, salt and savoury. Pho is a simple broth in which you poach vegetables, adding seasonings of your choosing. If you can find Thai basil, use it for an authentic taste. Omit the fish sauce for veggies.

Begin by preparing the pickles so that they can soak while you cook the pho soup. Using a swivel peeler, peel thin ribbons of the baby corn and carrots. Leave the skin on the cucumber, deseed and again peel the flesh into thin ribbons. In a bowl mix together the fish sauce, vinegar and sugar. Toss the vegetable ribbons in the pickling syrup and leave to pickle.

Peel and finely slice the ginger. In a large saucepan, fry the onion, garlic and ginger slices in the oil until the onion is soft. Add the star anise, cinnamon and dried hot pepper flakes to the pan and fry for a further minute. Add the coriander/cilantro, basil, soy sauce, fish sauce and stock and simmer for about 10 minutes. Finely slice the carrot into ribbons using a swivel peeler and add to the pan. Trim and finely slice the spring onions/scallions, trim the pak choi/bok choy and slice lengthways, slice the mushrooms and add them all to the pan. Pour in the lime juice, add the sugar and simmer for 5 minutes. Add the noodles and cook for a further 5 minutes. Remove the star anise and pour into bowls to serve, garnishing with a little more coriander/cilantro.

While the soup is cooking prepare the sandwiches. Add the olive oil to a griddle pan. Cut the tofu into eight slices and cook in the pan for 8–10 minutes until golden brown on both sides, turning halfway through. Add the sweet chilli/chili sauce to the pan and cook for a further minute to heat the sauce. Sprinkle over the fresh coriander/cilantro.

Cut the baguettes in two and slice along the top. Drain the pickles and place some in each sandwich together with two slices of the grilled tofu. Serve the sandwiches with the soup.

1 litre/quart chicken stock
140 g/5 oz. water chestnuts
2.5-cm/1-inch piece ginger,
    peeled and finely chopped
2 large oyster mushrooms
20 enoki mushrooms
1 garlic clove, finely chopped
2 tablespoons dark soy sauce
1 tablespoon fish sauce
1 red chilli/chile, finely sliced
    and deseeded
1 tablespoon tomato purée/
    paste
200 g/7 oz. cooked chicken
100 g/1 cup sugar snap peas,
    sliced
100 g/³/₄ cup frozen peas
3 spring onions/scallions
1 egg, beaten
2 tablespoons sherry vinegar
2 tablespoons cornflour/
    cornstarch

For the herb wraps
1 carrot, peeled and trimmed
15-cm/6-inch piece cucumber
4 tablespoons beansprouts
2 tablespoons chopped
    coriander/cilantro
juice of 1 lime
1 teaspoon white sugar
soy and fish sauces, to taste
¹/₄ teaspoon Chinese five
    spice powder
4 spring roll wrappers

Serves 4

Chinese hot and sour soup with herb wraps

This hot and sour soup has an amazing flavour and texture. I love enoki mushrooms – they look like something from a fairytale – but if you cannot find them you can substitute button mushrooms instead. The wraps are light and refreshing, filled with fresh vegetables and herbs.

For the soup, pour the stock into a saucepan and heat over a gentle heat. Slice the water chestnuts and add to the stock along with the ginger, mushrooms, garlic, soy sauce, fish sauce, sliced chilli/chile and tomato purée/paste. Simmer for about 5 minutes until the mushrooms are soft. Coarsely chop the chicken and add it to the pan along with the sugar snap peas, frozen peas and trimmed and finely sliced spring onions/scallions. Simmer for a further 5 minutes to allow the peas to cook. Very slowly pour the beaten egg into the soup in a thin line so that it cooks in small pieces in the soup. Mix the vinegar with the cornflour/cornstarch to make a smooth paste, then add in a ladleful of the stock from the soup (but without any of the solid ingredients) and whisk well to dissolve the cornflour/cornstarch. It is important to do this as if you just add the paste to the soup you can end up with lumps of cornflour/cornstarch jelly which ruin the soup. Whisk the cornflour/cornstarch liquid into the soup over the heat which will thicken it. Set aside until you are ready to serve.

For the wraps, finely slice the carrot and cucumber into strips about 5 cm/2 inches in length. Place in a bowl with the beansprouts and coriander/cilantro. Whisk together the lime juice, sugar, soy and fish sauces and five spice powder, then pour over the vegetables and toss lightly.

Soak the spring roll wrappers one at a time in warm water in a shallow dish for about 20 seconds. Spread out flat on a damp kitchen towel to drain. Prepare the rolls one at a time. Arrange a neat line of vegetables in the centre of a wrap and fold up one of the sides into the centre. Fold in both the sides which are at right angles to the side you have already folded. Fold the remaining side over to finish. Chill until you are ready to serve.

Reheat the soup, ladle into bowls and serve with the herb wraps on the side.

5 plum tomatoes

3 roasted red (bell) peppers in brine (such as Karyatis)

250 g/9 oz. strawberries

1 whole cucumber

2 spring onions/scallions

1/2 bulb fennel

a handful of fresh basil

1/2 teaspoon smoked paprika

30 ml/2 tablespoons white wine vinegar

75 ml/5 tablespoons olive oil, plus extra to drizzle

salt and pepper, to season

For the pickled peppers

1 red (bell) pepper

100 ml/1/3 cup white wine vinegar

1 tablespoon white sugar

For the tapenade toasts

4 slices sourdough bread

2 tablespoons black olive tapenade

8 slices serrano ham

50 g/2 oz. feta cheese, crumbled

a few small black olives

olive oil, to drizzle

Serves 4

Strawberry gazpacho with olive tapenade open sandwiches

My wonderful publisher and friend Julia Charles loves gazpacho and we often eat it in my garden in the sunshine when she comes to visit. It is perfect on hot days as it is so refreshing. The topping for the toasts is inspired by Julia's friend chef Bart Van Capellen, who shared his recipe for pickled peppers with her – they really bring this dish to life.

Cut the tomatoes in half and scoop out the seeds with a small spoon, then roughly chop the flesh. Chop the preserved (bell) peppers and place in a bowl with the tomatoes. Reserve a few of the strawberries for the garnish, then hull and chop the remainder and add to the bowl with the tomatoes. Trim the ends of the cucumber and peel off the skin with a swivel vegetable peeler. Cut the cucumber in half lengthways and deseed using a teaspoon. Cut into small pieces, reserving a little for garnish, and place the remainder in the bowl. Trim the ends from the spring onions/scallions and fennel and roughly chop. Add to the bowl together with the basil, paprika, vinegar and olive oil. Season with salt and pepper, cover and chill in the refrigerator for 3 hours or overnight.

To prepare the pickled peppers, trim away the stalk and deseed the (bell) pepper. Slice into very thin strips. In a bowl whisk together the vinegar and sugar with 100 ml/1/3 cup water until the sugar has dissolved. Add the sliced (bell) pepper and leave to soak for 1–2 hours, then drain away the pickling liquid.

Blitz the soup to a smooth purée in a blender or food processor. Taste for seasoning, adding a little more salt and pepper if needed.

Lightly toast the bread, spread with a little olive tapenade and top with slices of serrano ham. Sprinkle feta over the top. Finish each with slices of pickled pepper and olives and drizzle with olive oil and season with a little black pepper. To serve, pour the soup into bowls or glasses. Finely chop the reserved strawberries and cucumber and place a little in the centre of each serving. Drizzle with a little olive oil and serve straight away.

home-cooked comforts

Ingredients

1 small whole fresh chicken (approx. 1.35 kg/3 lb.)

2 large carrots, peeled and chopped

1 large leek, trimmed and finely sliced

125 ml/½ cup sweet sherry

1 onion, peeled and chopped

2 tablespoons freshly chopped tarragon leaves

2 teaspoons wholegrain mustard

2 spring onions/scallions

200 ml/generous ¾ cup white wine

125 g/4½ oz. thin dried egg noodles

salt and pepper, to season

For the rolls

1 tablespoon mayonnaise

2 tablespoons crème fraîche

2 teaspoons wholegrain mustard

1 tablespoon freshly chopped tarragon

grated zest of 1 lemon

salt and pepper, to season

4 rolls

Serves 4

Chicken noodle broth with lemon tarragon chicken rolls

This is a light broth, rich in chicken flavour with hints of aniseed from the tarragon. If you do not have time to boil the chicken, replace it with ready-cooked chicken and use a good-quality chicken stock instead.

Place the chicken in a large saucepan and add enough water to cover it. Add the carrots and leek to the pan with the sherry. Add the onion, season with salt and pepper and add 1 tablespoon of the chopped tarragon. Bring to the boil and then simmer the chicken for around 1 hour until the chicken is cooked and is starting to fall from the bone.

Carefully remove the chicken. Strain the soup (discarding the vegetables, but reserving the stock) and skim any fat from the surface. Simmer the stock for a further 20 minutes until it has reduced by one-third to intensify the flavours. Leave the chicken and stock to cool and then chill in the refrigerator. Remove any fat that has set on top of the stock.

Remove the chicken breasts from the cooled chicken and cut into slices and return to the refrigerator until you are ready to make the sandwiches. Remove the meat from the remainder of the chicken, discarding the bones and skin. Add the chicken to the stock in a saucepan and reheat, adding the mustard. Trim the spring onions/scallions and finely chop with the remaining tablespoon of tarragon and add to the pan with the white wine. Heat and then taste the soup for seasoning adding more salt and pepper to your taste.

To prepare the rolls, whisk together the mayonnaise, crème fraîche, mustard and tarragon. Stir in the lemon zest and season to taste. Fold the dressing through the chicken slices. Halve each roll and fill with a portion of the chicken. When you are ready to serve, add the noodles to the soup and simmer for around 3–5 minutes. Serve straight away.

1 onion, finely chopped
1 tablespoon olive oil
2.5-cm/1-inch piece of ginger
1 garlic clove, finely chopped
1 large red chilli/chile pepper
15 g/1 tablespoon butter
6 tomatoes
1 teaspoon smoked paprika
$^1/_2$ teaspoon cayenne pepper
1 teaspoon each ground
   cumin and cinnamon
$^1/_2$ teaspoon ground allspice
2 x 400-g/14-oz. cans black
   beans
800 ml/3$^1/_4$ cups vegetable or
   chicken stock
sprigs of coriander/cilantro
1 avocado, pitted and peeled
juice of 1 lime
4 tablespoons sour cream
salt and pepper, to season

For the muffins
150 g/1 cup fine cornmeal
30 g/4 tablespoons self-
   raising/self-rising flour
1 teaspoon bicarbonate of
   soda/baking soda
$^1/_4$ teaspoon hot paprika
300 ml/1$^3/_4$ cups buttermilk
20 g/1 tablespoon soft butter
1 egg
165 g/1 cup sweetcorn

a 12-hole muffin pan, greased

Serves 4

Costa Rican black bean soup with cornbread muffins

On a trip to Costa Rica I stayed at the most wonderful organic finca just outside San Jose called Finca Rosa Blanca. The food was all sourced locally and one of the highlights was their black bean soup. Here, my version is served with warm cornbread muffins on the side.

As the muffins are best served warm straight from the oven, you can begin by preparing these as they will bake while you make the soup. Preheat the oven to 190°C (375°F) Gas 5.

Place the cornmeal (or fine polenta), flour, bicarbonate of soda/baking soda, paprika, buttermilk, butter and egg in a mixing bowl and whisk together until smooth. Fold in the sweetcorn and season with salt and pepper. Place the cornbread mixture into eight of the holes of the muffin pan. Bake in the preheated oven for 30–35 minutes, until the muffins are golden brown on top. Remove from the oven and keep warm.

For the soup, sauté the onion in a little olive oil in a pan. Peel and finely chop the ginger and add to the pan along with the garlic. Sauté until the garlic is lightly golden brown. Deseed the pepper and chop into small pieces. Reserve a few pieces of pepper for garnish and add the remainder to the pan with the butter. Cook until the pepper starts to soften. Blitz the tomatoes in a blender or food processor to a smooth purée/paste. Add the paprika, cayenne pepper, cumin, cinnamon and allspice to the pan and fry in the oil for a minute to release the flavours. Drain and rinse the black beans and add to the pan with the stock and tomatoes. Simmer for about 20–30 minutes, then season with salt and pepper to taste and stir in some chopped coriander/cilantro leaves.

Chop the avocado into small pieces and toss in the lime juice to prevent it discolouring.

Pour the warm soup into bowls and top each with a spoonful of sour cream, some avocado pieces and the reserved peppers. Serve with the warm muffins on the side.

400 ml/scant 1¾ cups
    coconut milk
200 g/generous 1 cup red
    split lentils
1 large red chilli/chile
4 large vine tomatoes
2.5-cm/1-inch piece of ginger,
    peeled and finely chopped
1 teaspoon fenugreek
1 tablespoon garam masala
salt and pepper, to season

For the stuffed naan
4 rashers/strips rindless
    streaky/fatty bacon
1 tablespoon olive oil
1 small onion, peeled and
    finely sliced
1 green chilli/chile, peeled
    and finely sliced
1 teaspoon garam masala
½ teaspoon ground
    cinnamon
3 eggs
salt and pepper, to season
2 large naan breads

For the tadka
2 tablespoons ghee or
    clarified butter
1 large garlic clove, finely
    sliced
6 curry leaves
1 tablespoon black onion/
    nigella seeds

Serves 4

Spiced lentil soup with stuffed naan

This soup is inspired by my good friend Steven Wallis, winner of UK Masterchef in 2007 and an all-round amazing chef who cooks the best curries I know. It is a subtly spiced Indian dhal with coconut, finished with a tadka (spiced butter) and served with a tasty stuffed naan.

For the soup, heat 800 ml/generous 3¼ cups water and the coconut milk in a large saucepan and pour in the lentils and a pinch of salt. Cut a slit in the chilli/chile but keep it whole as you will remove it later. Halve the tomatoes and add to the pan with the ginger, fenugreek and garam masala. Simmer for about 30 minutes until the lentils are soft. Remove the chilli/chile and discard it. Transfer the soup to a blender or food processor and blitz until smooth. Return to the pan and season well with salt and pepper.

For the stuffed naan, cut the bacon into small pieces and fry in a little olive oil until crisp. Remove from the pan, leaving some of the fat in the pan and set aside. Add the onion to the pan and fry until it starts to turn translucent. Add the sliced chilli/chile to the pan and fry for a few minutes more. Add the garam masala and cinnamon and return the bacon to the pan. Season with salt and pepper. Whisk the eggs and then pour into the pan, swirling so that the onion and bacon are evenly distributed. Cook the omelette/omelet until the egg is just cooked through. While the omelette/omelet is cooking, warm the naan bread. Place the omelette/omelet on top of one of the naans. Top with the second naan and press down, then cut into quarters.

To prepare the tadka (it is best to do this while the omelette/omelet is cooking so that everything is ready at the same time), heat the ghee in a small frying pan/skillet or saucepan then add the garlic, curry leaves and black onion/nigella seeds and fry until the garlic just starts to turn golden brown. Take care that it does not burn. Pour the soup, reheated if it has cooled, into four bowls and then top each with a spoonful of the tadka, which your guests should stir into the soup. Serve straight away with the stuffed naan. The soup will keep for up to 3 days in an airtight container in the refrigerator. The naan should be eaten as soon as it is made.

Moroccan chickpea soup with falafel and harissa pockets

3 shallots, finely chopped

15 g/1 tablespoon butter

1 tablespoon olive oil

1 garlic clove, finely sliced

1 teaspoon black onion/
nigella seeds

1 teaspoon ground cinnamon

juice of 2 lemons

1 teaspoon rose harissa

2 x 400-g/14-oz. cans cooked
chickpeas/garbanzo beans,
drained

80 g/$\frac{1}{2}$ cup soft dried
apricots

1 litre/quart chicken or
vegetable stock

black pepper, to season

fennel fronds, to garnish
(optional)

For the falafel pockets

1 teaspoon rose harissa

200 g/1 cup Greek yogurt

12 ready-made falafels

4 wholemeal pitta pockets

a few handfuls of mixed soft
salad leaves

salt and pepper, to season

Serves 4

I love exploring the souks of Marrakech and admiring the amazing spice towers, the air filled with delicious aromas. Moroccan food is so flavoursome with hints of cinnamon and citrus as well as fiery heat. My favourite harissa is made with rose petals (Belazu make a wonderful one) but if you cannot find it, substitute regular harissa paste instead.

For the soup, fry the shallots in the butter and olive oil until the shallots are soft and translucent. Add the garlic and fry until lightly golden brown. Add the black onion/nigella seeds and cinnamon and fry for a minute to heat the spices, stirring all the time. Add the lemon juice, harissa, chickpeas/garbanzo beans, apricots and stock to the pan and simmer for about 20 minutes. Pour the soup into a blender or food processor and blitz until smooth. Return to the pan and keep warm.

To make the harissa yogurt dressing for the falafel pockets, fold the harissa into the Greek yogurt, season with salt and pepper to your taste, cover and store in the refrigerator until you are ready to serve.

When ready to serve, preheat the oven to the temperature recommended on the falafel packaging and cook the falafel following the package instructions. Warm the pitta breads under the grill/broiler and then cut them open. Fill each with salad leaves and falafel and top with a drizzle of the harissa yogurt dressing.

Pour the soup into bowls and top with chopped fennel fronds, if using, and freshly ground black pepper. Serve straight away with the falafel pockets on the side.

Sweet red pepper, fennel and ouzo soup with prawn/shrimp saganaki pittas

2 onions, finely sliced

2 garlic cloves, finely sliced

1–2 tablespoons olive oil

1 bulb of fennel, trimmed

3 sweet red (bell) peppers, deseeded and chopped

75 ml/5 tablespoons ouzo

300 g/10$^{1}/_{2}$ oz. passata/strained tomatoes

600 ml/2$^{1}/_{2}$ cups chicken or vegetable stock

salt and pepper, to season

For the prawn/shrimp pittas

200 g/7 oz. feta cheese

60 ml/$^{1}/_{4}$ cup ouzo

200 g/7 oz. passata/strained tomatoes

1 tablespoon freshly chopped mint leaves

225 g/8 oz. raw prawns/shrimp, shells removed

1 tablespoon olive oil

4 white pitta pockets

Serves 4

On a trip to Cyprus our hotel served prawn saganaki and I loved it so much that I ordered it almost every night! It had a delicious aniseed flavour as it was cooked with ouzo and was sprinkled with salty feta cheese. It is the inspiration for this deliciously summery soup.

In a saucepan, sauté the onions and garlic in 1 tablespoon of the olive oil, until softened and the onions start to caramelize. Stir all the time to ensure they do not burn. Put half of the onions and garlic in an ovenproof dish and set aside.

Chop most of the fennel, reserving a piece to peel into ribbons for the garnish as well as any fronds, and add to the onions with the (bell) peppers and a little more olive oil if needed. Sauté until the (bell) peppers and fennel soften, stirring frequently. Add the ouzo and cook for 1 minute. Add the passata/strained tomatoes and stock and season with salt and pepper. Simmer for about 15–20 minutes.

Pour the soup into a blender or food processor and blitz until very smooth. Season to taste. Set aside while you prepare the pittas.

Preheat the oven to 180°C (350°F) Gas 4. For the saganaki sauce, crumble the feta on top of the reserved onions and pour over the ouzo and the 200 g/7 oz. of passata/strained tomatoes. Sprinkle with the mint and bake in the oven for 15–20 minutes until the cheese is soft.

While the cheese is baking, in a hot frying pan/skillet or wok, pan fry the prawns/shrimp in 1 tablespoon of olive oil for 3–5 minutes until the prawns/shrimp have turned a deep pink colour and are slightly golden around the edges. Place a large spoonful of the saganaki sauce into each pitta and fill with the prawns/shrimp. Pour the soup into bowls. Using a swivel vegetable peeler, peel thin ribbons of the reserved fennel and use to garnish the soup, along with any fennel fronds, drizzling with a little extra olive oil. Serve straight away.

Horseradish borscht with whipped cream cheese and chive on rye

450 g/1 lb. fresh beetroot/
   beets
2 onions
1–2 tablespoons olive oil
100 g/3$^1/_2$ oz. new potatoes
   or white potatoes
1 cooking apple
juice of 2 oranges
1 tablespoon creamed
   horseradish sauce
800 ml/generous 3$^1/_4$ cups
   beef or vegetable stock
salt and pepper, to season
cream, to swirl (optional)

For the rye toasts
100 g/$^1/_2$ cup cream cheese
50 ml/3$^1/_2$ tablespoons
   natural/plain yogurt
1 tablespoon finely chopped/
   snipped chives, plus extra
   to garnish
4 slices dark rye bread
black pepper

Serves 4

Beetroot/beets make one of the most amazing coloured soups I know. This one is delicately flavoured with orange and apple and a kick of horseradish. Served with dark rye bread open sandwiches topped with a creamy chive cheese, this earthy soup is good for the soul.

Preheat the oven to 180°C (350°F) Gas 4.

Begin by peeling the beetroot/beets and onions and then chop both the onion and beetroot/beets into wedges and place in a roasting pan. Drizzle with a little olive oil and season with salt and pepper. Roast for about 30 minutes until the beetroot/beets are just soft. If the onions start to brown before the beetroot/beets are cooked, remove them from the oven and set aside until the beetroot/beets are ready. You can tell they are cooked when a sharp knife slides out easily.

Place the roasted beetroot/beets and onions in a large saucepan. If you are using new potatoes, cut them in half and place in the pan without removing the skins. If you are using larger white potatoes, peel them and cut into pieces and place in the pan. Peel and core the apple, chop it into pieces and add to the pan. Add the orange juice, horseradish and stock to the pan and simmer for about 20–30 minutes until the potatoes are soft.

Pour the soup into a blender or food processor and blitz to a smooth purée. Return to the pan and keep warm until you are ready to serve.

For the rye toasts, whisk the cream cheese and yogurt until thick and smooth in a mixing bowl. Stir in the chopped/snipped chives. Lightly toast the rye bread. Spread the cream cheese mixture over the slices of rye, decorate with some extra chives and sprinkle with a little freshly ground black pepper. Pour the soup into bowls, swirl a drizzle of cream over the top if using and serve with the rye toasts.

1 tablespoon coconut oil
1 tablespoon tom yum paste
2 tablespoons dark soy sauce
2 tablespoons fish sauce
1 tablespoon brown sugar
juice of 3 limes
2 very large tomatoes
200 ml/^{3}/$_4$ cup coconut milk
250 g/9 oz. chestnut
    mushrooms
1 red chilli/chile, finely sliced
2 spring onions/scallions,
    finely sliced
a handful of Thai basil leaves
    and coriander/cilantro
225 g/8 oz. raw/uncooked
    king prawns/jumbo shrimp
black pepper, to season

For the satay sauce
125 ml/^{1}/$_2$ cup coconut milk
2 tablespoons peanut butter
juice of 1 lime
1 tablespoon each fish sauce,
    soy sauce and brown sugar
^{1}/$_2$ tablespoon tamarind
    paste

For the flatbreads
2 skinless chicken breasts
1 tablespoon olive oil
4 flatbreads
1 tablespoon salted peanuts
coriander/cilantro leaves
black pepper, to season

Serves 4

Thai hot and spicy coconut soup with chicken satay flatbreads

This soup is hot and spicy with a real kick. Thai 'tom yum' paste is a readily available ingredient and adds real flavour here. You'll need to use a soft dark brown sugar for this recipe and try to find Thai basil for authenticity. The nutty chicken satay is the perfect accompaniment.

For the soup, heat the coconut oil (or olive oil) in a large saucepan, add the tom yum paste and fry over a gentle heat quickly. Add 1 litre/quart water to the pan together with the soy sauce, fish sauce, sugar and lime juice. Cut the tomatoes into slim wedges and add to the pan and pour in the coconut milk. Simmer until warm. Clean and trim the mushrooms, cut them in half and add to the pan, then simmer until they are soft. Add the sliced chilli/chile and spring onions/scallions, basil and coriander/cilantro.

Just before you are ready to serve the soup, cut a slit along the back of each prawn/shrimp (do not cut all the way through – you just want to cut a slit deep enough so that the prawns/shrimp curl up when they are cooked), discard any black tracts and add to the pan. Simmer for a few minutes until the prawns/shrimp are pink and cooked through. Season with a little black pepper if you wish. There should be sufficient salt from the fish sauce and soy sauce, but taste and season again if you wish.

For the flatbreads, begin by preparing the satay sauce. Place the coconut milk in a saucepan with the peanut butter and whisk over a gentle heat until smooth. Add the lime juice, fish and soy sauces, sugar and tamarind paste and whisk until everything is incorporated. Set aside.

Chop the chicken into small pieces and fry in a pan with the oil for 6–8 minutes until lightly golden brown and cooked through. Stir in the satay sauce and simmer gently for a few minutes. Warm the flatbreads. To serve, pour the soup into bowls. Place the flatbreads onto plates and top each with a generous spoonful of the satay chicken. Roughly chop the peanuts and sprinkle over with the coriander/cilantro leaves. Season with black pepper and serve.

indulgent treats

1 kg/2 lb. whole langoustines

2 tablespoons olive oil

2 onions, finely chopped

1 garlic clove, finely chopped

1 stick/rib celery, chopped

4 carrots, finely chopped

2 sprigs of thyme

60 g/$^1/_2$ stick butter

75 ml/5 tablespoons brandy, plus a dash for the soup

160 ml/$^3/_4$ cup Noilly Prat

2 large tomatoes, quartered

1 tablespoon tomato purée/paste

400-g/14-oz. can tomatoes

500 ml/2 cups fish stock

juice of 1 lemon

200 ml/generous $^3/_4$ cup double/heavy cream

salt and pepper, to season

For the rolls

50 g/3$^1/_2$ tablespoons butter

200 g/7 oz. cooked prawns/shrimp

4 crusty bread rolls, split

flat-leaf parsley and snipped/chopped chives, to garnish

lemon wedges, for squeezing

Serves 4

Langoustine bisque with seafood rolls

This is a rich soup with a really intense flavour, which comes from roasting the shells of the langoustines before putting them into the soup. The rolls are simply filled with delicious buttered seafood.

Bring a large stockpot of salted water to the boil. Add the langoustines and simmer for about 5 minutes until cooked (the meat under the tail should have turned white). Place into cold water to chill and then peel away the shells. Remove the head and tail, peel the shell from the body and remove the black intestinal tract. Reserve the shells. Chill the langoustine flesh until needed. Preheat the oven to 200°C (400°F) Gas 6.

Place the langoustine heads and shells in a large roasting pan, drizzle with 1 tablespoon of the olive oil and season. Roast for 20–30 minutes until the shells turn light golden brown. Meanwhile, add the onions, garlic, celery and carrots to a large saucepan with the remaining 1 tablespoon olive oil and the thyme. Gently sauté for 10–15 minutes until the vegetables soften. Remove from the pan and set aside.

Tip the roasted shells into a clean saucepan, add 50 g/3½ tablespoons of the butter and fry for a few minutes. Add the brandy and Noilly Prat and cook for 2 minutes. Add the fresh tomatoes along with the onion, garlic, celery and carrot mixture, the tomato purée/paste, canned tomatoes, fish stock and 1 litre/quart water. Season. Cook for 1½ hours over a gentle heat, then pass the soup through a fine mesh sieve/strainer or muslin in batches. Return the soup to the pan and add the lemon juice and cream. To finish the soup add the remaining 10 g/2 teaspoons butter, an extra dash of brandy and heat through.

For the rolls, melt the butter, then toss the prawns/shrimp and langoustine flesh in the warm melted butter. Stir through the herbs, lemon juice and black pepper and spoon into the rolls. Serve immediately.

Chilled avocado soup with smoked salmon and whipped cream cheese bagels

4 avocados, halved, stoned/
   pitted and peeled
juice of 2 lemons
400 ml/scant 1³/₄ cups
   vegetable stock
200 ml/generous ³/₄ cup
   single/light cream
1 tablespoon dill, plus extra
   to garnish
salt and pepper, to season
olive oil, to drizzle

For the bagels
4 bagels, halved
120 g/4 oz. smoked salmon
140 g/5 oz. whipped
   cream cheese (sold in
   supermarkets)
grated zest of lemon
cracked black pepper,
   to season

Serves 4

On summer days there is nothing nicer to serve for an appetizer or lunch in the sunshine than this chilled soup with creamy smoked salmon bagels. This soup has a thick and luxurious consistency, perfect for dipping your bagel into. It is rich, so serve small bowlfuls.

Chop half of one avocado into small pieces and drizzle with the juice of one of the lemons to prevent it discolouring. Set aside for the garnish.

Place the remaining avocado in a blender or food processor with the stock, cream, the juice of the remaining lemon and the dill and blend to a smooth purée. Season with salt and pepper to taste.

Lightly toast the bagels. Chop half of the smoked salmon into small pieces and mix into the cream cheese with the lemon zest and some freshly ground pepper. There is no need to add salt as the salmon is salty enough. Spread the salmon cream cheese mixture over the bottom half of the bagels. Divide the remaining salmon into four slices and place on top of the cream cheese mixture and cover with the bagel tops.

Pour the soup into four bowls and garnish with the reserved lemon-coated avocado, sprigs of dill, some coarse ground black pepper and a drizzle of olive oil. Serve straight away while the bagels are still warm.

Clam chowder with fennel salad crispbreads

1 kg/2 lb. 4 oz. fresh clams
150 ml/²/₃ cup Noilly Prat
500 g/1 lb. 2 oz. white
   potatoes, peeled and
   chopped into small pieces
200 g/7 oz. diced pancetta
1 tablespoon olive oil
1 onion, sliced
30 g/2 tablespoons butter
2 tablespoons plain/
   all-purpose flour
250 ml/1 cup milk
250 ml/1 cup double/heavy
   cream

For the salad dressing
1 teaspoon wholegrain
   mustard
juice of 1 lemon
1 tablespoon olive oil
1 teaspoon white sugar
salt and pepper, to season

For the crispbreads
2 handfuls of lamb's lettuce
   and pea shoots
¹/₄ bulb of fennel, peeled into
   thin ribbons
4 tablespoons cream cheese
4 thin crispbreads

Serves 4

I have fond memories of eating clam chowder at a seafood restaurant in Boston, where everyone sat together on long tables. It was a fun evening and the soup was delicious. Clam chowder is very rich and really needs very little on the side so I have paired it here with a salad-topped crispbread with fresh fennel to cut through all the cream.

This recipe uses fresh clams and it is important to cook them carefully to ensure that you do not use any dead clams. (If you prefer, you can substitute canned clams in the US, but these are not readily available in the UK.) Rinse the shells and check that they all close. Discard any open clams. Place the clams in a pan with 250 ml/1 cup water and the Noilly Prat and cook for 6–8 minutes. The clam shells should open. Remove all opened clams from the pan and cook the remaining clams for a further 2–3 minutes. Discard any clams that remain closed. Remove the clams from their shells and set aside in the refrigerator while you prepare the soup. Reserve the cooking liquid but strain it through a fine mesh sieve/strainer to remove any impurities.

Cook the potatoes in plenty of salted boiling water until just soft. Drain from the water and set aside.

In a large saucepan cook the pancetta in the olive oil until crisp. Remove from the pan and fry the onion in the pan until it is soft and translucent. Return the pancetta to the pan with the potatoes and cook for a few minutes more. Melt the butter in the pan and stir in the flour. Cook for a few minutes. Add the clam cooking liquid to the pan, straining it again before adding. Simmer for a few minutes, then add the milk and cream and season to taste. If the soup is too thick add a little more milk or water to loosen. Simmer for 10 minutes, then stir through the reserved clams.

Whisk together the dressing ingredients and then gently toss the salad leaves in the dressing. Add the fennel ribbons to the salad. Spread a spoonful of cream cheese onto each of the crispbreads and top with a generous serving of the salad. Spoon the soup into bowls and serve straight away with the crispbreads.

Butternut squash soup with Thanksgiving pretzel sandwiches

2 onions, finely chopped
1 tablespoon olive oil
1 teaspoon garam masala
1 tablespoon black onion/
  nigella seeds
1/2 teaspoon ground
  cinnamon
pinch of cayenne pepper
900 g/2 lb. butternut squash,
  peeled, deseeded and
  chopped into chunks
800 ml/generous 3 1/4 cups
  chicken or vegetable stock
black pepper

For the pretzels
4 large soft pretzels
2–3 spoonfuls mayonnaise
4 large slices turkey
4 tablespoons cranberry
  sauce
4 slices Swiss cheese

Serves 4

After all the festivities of Thanksgiving or Christmas, there are often some slices of turkey and some cranberry sauce left over. I love to serve these in pretzel sandwiches, similar to those I have enjoyed on trips to Bavaria, but if you can't find pretzels, thick-cut slices of white bread are equally delicious. Using seasonal butternut squash, this spicy soup makes a pleasant change the day after Thanksgiving or Christmas day.

Place the onions in a large saucepan with the oil and cook over a gentle heat until the onions are soft and translucent. Add the garam masala, black onion/nigella seeds, cinnamon and cayenne pepper. If you do not like spicy soup, then omit the cayenne pepper. Fry for a few minutes further to allow the spices to heat. Add the squash to the pan and cook for a few minutes, then add the stock and simmer for about 30 minutes until the squash is soft.

Pour the soup into the blender or food processor and blitz until smooth. Keep warm until you are ready to serve.

For the sandwiches, carefully slice each pretzel in half horizontally and spread each half with a little mayonnaise. Place a slice of turkey on each base and top with some cranberry sauce. Add slices of Swiss cheese and cover each with the pretzel tops. (If you wish, you can toast the pretzels until the cheese starts to melt.) Divide the soup into warm bowls, sprinkle with freshly ground black pepper and serve straight away with the sandwiches on the side.

2 onions, chopped
2 carrots, chopped
1 garlic clove
30 g/2 tablespoons butter
1 tablespoon olive oil
1 heaped tablespoon plain/
    all-purpose flour
400 ml/scant 1³/₄ cups beer
600 ml/2¹/₂ cups chicken or
    vegetable stock
1 teaspoon creamed
    horseradish sauce
¹/₂-1 teaspoon hot sauce,
    to taste
250 ml/1 cup double/heavy
    cream
2 tablespoons sour cream
100 g/3¹/₂ oz. cream cheese
125 g/4¹/₂ oz. cheddar
    cheese, grated
salt and pepper, to season

For the quesadillas
4 tortillas
200 g/7 oz. queso fresco
1 large avocado, halved,
    stoned/pitted and peeled
juice of 1 lime
1–2 tablespoons jalapeño
    chillies/chiles

Serves 4

Cheese and beer soup with avocado, queso fresco and jalapeño quesadillas

This is an indulgent soup with a fiery kick. It is rich with cream and cheese and has delicious undertones of hops from the beer. If you cannot find queso fresco, whisk together equal parts of feta cheese and cream cheese until smooth and use instead.

In a large saucepan, sauté the onions, carrots and garlic in the butter and olive oil until the onions are soft and translucent. Take care the garlic does not burn and stir all the time. Add the flour to the pan and cook for a minute, then add the beer and stock to the pan and simmer for about 5 minutes. Add the horseradish, hot sauce, double/heavy cream and sour cream, cream cheese and the cheddar cheese. Stir until all the cheese has melted. Blitz the soup in a blender or food processor until very smooth, then return to the pan. Taste for seasoning and add a little salt and pepper if needed. Keep warm until you are ready to serve.

For the quesadillas, place two of the tortillas on a large chopping board. Dot each with spoonfuls of the queso fresco. Mash the avocado with a fork with the lime juice to prevent it discolouring. Place spoonfuls of the avocado over the tortillas amongst the cheese and sprinkle with the jalapeños. Only use a few if you do not like much heat or omit them completely if you prefer. Top each with a second tortilla and press down gently with your hands.

Place one of the tortillas in a hot frying pan/skillet and heat for about 3–4 minutes, turning halfway through and taking care that it does not burn. You do not need to add any oil to the pan as you are just cooking to toast the tortillas rather than to fry them. Repeat with the other tortilla and then remove from the pan and cut each into quarters.

Pour the soup into bowls, sprinkle with extra black pepper and serve two quarters of tortilla with each portion.

White bean and pancetta soup with mini roasted vegetable picnic loaves

1 small white onion, finely
   chopped
1 tablespoon olive oil
200 g/7 oz. pancetta cubes
1 garlic clove, finely chopped
4 sprigs of thyme
400-g/14-oz. can cooked
   cannellini beans, drained
125 ml/^{1}/$_2$ cup Marsala wine
800 ml/generous 3^1/$_4$ cups
   chicken stock
salt and pepper, to season

For the picnic loaves
2 aubergines/eggplants
olive oil, to drizzle
juice of 1 lemon
4 small ciabatta rolls
4 flame-roasted (bell)
   peppers, preserved in
   brine, rinsed and patted
   dry on paper towels
a handful of baby spinach
   leaves

Serves 4

This soup transports me to the Tuscan hills where cannellini bean soup is popular lunchtime fare. Adding thyme and pancetta gives it a wonderful smoky flavour. The accompanying stuffed mini picnic loaves are perfect for summer eating, packed with delicious antipasti-style roasted (bell) peppers and aubergines/eggplants.

Preheat the oven to 180°C (350°F) Gas 4.

Begin by preparing the aubergine/eggplant for the picnic loaves. Trim the ends away and cut into slices about 1 cm/⅜ inch thick. Place in a roasting pan, drizzle generously with olive oil and roast for 30 minutes until the aubergines/eggplants are golden brown. Leave to cool in the roasting oil. Squeeze over the lemon juice and store in the refrigerator until needed.

For the soup, fry the onion in the olive oil until it is soft and translucent. Add the pancetta, garlic and sprigs of thyme to the pan and fry until the pancetta is cooked and starts to turn slightly golden brown. Stir all the time to make sure that it does not burn. Rinse the beans and then add to the pan and cook for 5 minutes so that the beans absorb the flavours of the oil. Remove two generous spoonfuls of the beans and pancetta and place in a small bowl. Remove the thyme from the pan, strip the leaves from the stalks and add to the bowl. Toss in a little olive oil and set aside.

Pour in the Marsala wine and the chicken stock and simmer for 15 minutes, or longer if you wish. Season with salt and pepper if needed, but I generally find the soup has enough salt from the pancetta. Blitz in a blender or food processor to a smooth purée.

For the loaves, cut the tops off the rolls and pull out the centre of the bread. (You can blitz into crumbs and freeze.) Line the bottom of each one with a few spinach leaves, then layer with aubergine/eggplant and (bell) peppers until the holes are full. Top with the lids. Pour the soup into bowls and garnish with the reserved beans, pancetta and thyme. Serve with the loaves on the side.

1 onion, finely chopped

1 garlic clove, finely chopped

1 tablespoon olive oil

450 g/1 lb. jar of roasted red (bell) peppers preserved in brine

250 g/9 oz. passata/strained tomatoes

800 ml/generous 3¹/₄ cups chicken or vegetable stock

2 teaspoons smoked paprika

4 tablespoons sour cream

fresh basil, finely chopped

salt and pepper, to season

For the meatball subs

12 fresh meatballs

1 small onion, finely sliced

1 tablespoon olive oil

60 ml/¹/₄ cup sherry

250 g/9 oz. passata/strained tomatoes

4 sub rolls

4 tablespoons grated cheddar cheese

a handful of fresh basil leaves

6–8 jalapeño chilli/chile slices

salt and pepper, to season

Serves 4

Goulash pepper soup with meatball subs

Goulash is the national dish of Hungary and a very good dish it is, too! Traditionally made with beef, it has a gently paprika-spiced sauce finished with sour cream. This is my version – a (bell) pepper soup and a beef meatball sub on the side – delicious topped with sour cream, grated cheese and jalapeños.

Start by preparing the meatball subs. Cook the meatballs following the packet instructions. For the sauce, fry the onion in the olive oil and sauté until soft and just starting to caramelize, stirring all the time. Add the sherry and simmer until it has reduced by half. Add the passata/strained tomatoes and simmer until the sauce thickens. Season with salt and pepper. Keep warm until you are ready to serve, or reheat before serving.

For the soup, add the onion and garlic to a saucepan with the olive oil and sauté until soft and just turning light golden brown. Drain the roasted (bell) peppers and rinse them. Cut a few thin slices of the (bell) pepper and reserve for garnish. Coarsely chop the remaining (bell) pepper, add to the pan and sauté for a few minutes. Add the passata/strained tomatoes, stock and smoked paprika and simmer for about 20 minutes.

Transfer to a blender or food processor and blitz until very smooth. Return to the pan and heat through. Season to taste with salt and pepper.

To finish the sandwiches, cut the sub rolls in half lengthways and add a layer of basil leaves. Place some of the warm meatballs in each roll and spoon over the warm meatball sauce. Sprinkle with grated cheese, which will melt in the heat of the sauce. Top with a few jalapeño chillies/chiles.

Pour the soup into bowls and top each with a spoonful of sour cream. Garnish with the reserved thin strips of the pepper and sprinkle with a little fresh basil. Serve straight away with a meatball sub alongside each bowl of soup.

Index